Rick,
     May you   s
of remembering   l
to be and compc   ~ roaay.
Lots of love always.
                    Pauline
                     xoxoxo

THE
Archive Photographs
SERIES

THE CITY OF
GLOUCESTER

Ye olde draperie shoppe, Waterloo house, Eastgate Street, was established in 1821 and is seen here in c.1890. It was pulled down to make way for Lloyds Bank.

THE
Archive Photographs
SERIES

THE CITY OF
GLOUCESTER

Compiled by
Jill Voyce

CHALFORD

First published 1995
Copyright © Jill Voyce, 1995

The Chalford Publishing Company
St Mary's Mill, Chalford,
Stroud, Gloucestershire, GL6 8NX

ISBN 0 7524 0306 0

Typesetting and origination by
The Chalford Publishing Company
Printed in Great Britain by
Redwood Books, Trowbridge

Contents

Introduction

In this, my third book of historical photographs of Gloucester City, I have again endeavoured to provide pictures which have not been published previously. Compiling this book has given me great pleasure and in my search for new material I have made new and reinforced old friendships. Anthony Done has again proved a great help and I am pleased to recognise his research and generosity. So many people have loaned me individual pictures and shared with me their memories and anecdotes. Names like Barton Gates will mean little to children and teenagers today but mention them to older Gloucestrians and memories of steam and diesel trains, traffic hold-ups and thriving railway carriage works follow. I especially liked the story about a well-known funeral director leading on foot a cortège down Barton Street (today renamed Eastgate Street). As soon as he crossed the railway lines the gates came down, barring the route to the cortège. The funeral director, however, is reported to have continued on his solemn way alone and quite unaware of what had happened. And those shoppers who were much amused by sale notices placed to attract custom – 'Rumsey's trousers down again, lower than ever.' It is such a shame that we have lost so many family businesses. Remember Alger and Blackmore, Winfield's, Blinkhorn's, Foyles, Staites, Southerns, Denton's – a glimpse of each will be found in this book. I regret the loss of individuality in both buildings and names within the city – especially pub names such as the Union, the Pelican, the Tabard, the British Flag and Northend Vaults. And the nursery rhyme quoted overleaf gives a very good reason for retaining the old name of Oxbody rather than the modern Oxbode.

Our ancient city has changed a great deal and not always to advantage. I live in hope that restoration and renewal of old properties is sympathetic to their surroundings and to their history, and that this book may help encourage this view.

Oxbode (pronounced Oxbody) Lane

There's an ox lying dead at the end of the lane,
His head on the pathway, his feet in the drain.
The lane is so narrow, his back was so wide,
He got stuck in the road 'twixt a house on each side.

He couldn't go forward, he couldn't go back,
He was stuck just as tight as a nail in a crack,
And the people all shouted, 'So tightly he fits
We must kill him and carve him and move him in bits.'

So a butcher despatched him and then had a sale
Of his ribs and his sirloin, his rump and his tail;
And the farmer he told me, 'I'll never again
Drive cattle to market down Oxbode Lane.'

From *Nursery Rhymes of Gloucester City* by E.P.R. Berryman (Bellows, 1950)

One

Streets

Outside Winfield's shop in Westgate Street 1906.

Westgate Street. The shop with five lamps is Fisher's drapery (today the Bank of Scotland). In 1869 F.W. Fisher founded the Gloucester branch and the family continued in business here until 1974, when after a short period on the corner of College Court, they moved to Southgate Street. Today Anthony Fisher has his business in Brunswick Road. There can be very few such long-standing family businesses remaining in Gloucester.

The horse-drawn cab is passing College Court c.1893.

Westgate Street in the 1890's - a century ago. It makes me realise just how long Olivers, Alger and Blackmore the grate people and Winfield's seed merchants served Gloucester's needs.

A little lower down Westgate Street c.1910.

Bull Lane c.1880. With the current interest in the National Lottery it is perhaps pertinent to record a report of 1771 from the Gloucester Journal. When Mr Hincks of the Bull Inn shared a first prize in the National Lottery he 'treated his friends and customers with great generosity and rubbed out all the scores' (wiped the slate clean).

Bull Lane c.1887-8. Lamerton cabinet makers were in Bull Lane for only two years according to the directories which gives us a fairly precise date for this photograph.

Westgate Street opposite the Shire Hall in the 1890's. What wonderful timber-framed houses we have lost!

Westgate Street 1938.

Westgate Street just before the war. Fortunately little has changed today, except for the traffic.

Westgate Street c.1930. The three shops stood on what is today the frontage of Fountain Square.

These buildings survived until 1971 when they were replaced by the Dukeries. They were the White Swan, Eagle House, or the Duke of Norfolk's lodging as it is usually known, the entrance to Co-operative buildings, one of many courtyards off Westgate Street, and Satis, with a sign for Bibby's animal feeds. I am told that the house and cart belonged to Doris Pinkney, a second-hand goods dealer.

Lower Westgate Street opposite St Bartholomew's almshouses (now Westgate Galleria) in the 1890's.

St Mary's Square. This picture was taken in about 1907 from the tower of St Mary de Lode church. The monument to Bishop Hooper can be seen facing St Mary's gate, but, with one exception, all the fine houses in the area were demolished in the 1960s for the Fountain Square development.

Deans Walk from the corner of St Catherine Street c.1907. This was before the council houses in Deans Way were built. Gloucester RFC supporters will recognise the way to the Kingsholm ground. The iron railings were taken away at the outbreak of World War II, like many others around the country.

St Catherine's Knapp c.1918. On the timber-framed building a plaque reminds us that the first Sunday School for girls was established here. Milk deliveries were made to households with horse-drawn floats, like the one on the left. Milk was dispensed from churns into jugs on the doorsteps. The horse droppings were usually collected by people for garden fertilizer.

Hare Lane looking towards the Knapp c. 1880. A lovely old picture showing a street of great character - contrast today's scene!

Kingsholm Road viewed from the bottom of Denmark Road, an old toll house and tram on the left. The house on the extreme right was the residence of Mr W.H. Colborn, who sent this postcard to his daughter in France in 1926. Old Centralians will remember Miss Colborn was one of the teachers.

This was photographed in 1906 and is still easily recognisable today. This is Kingsholm Road, with the rugby ground on the left and the Kingsholm Inn just above the entry to Sweetbriar Street on the right.

Kingsholm Square before the First World War.

The top end of Alvin Street in the late 1950s. The photographer was facing towards London Road with Sherbourne Street to his left.

This picture reflects a pace of life long gone, when the boys of the National School could stand in London Road to watch a photographer c.1912. On the left are the frontages of Duggan, boot-repairer, Fream, the builders and the railings of Northgate House are clearly seen. On the right is the Church Army hostel and large sign for the Great Western Railway goods depot.

A little further down London Road at the junction with Oxford Street 1963.

Northgate Street from London Road, Gloucester

The sun shining through George Street and Market Parade in about 1919 illuminates buildings lost in 1966 before the construction of the inner relief road. From the right we see the shop of E.T. Taylor, gilder and picture-frame maker, the Market Hotel, also I believe the meeting place for the Gloucester City Rifle Club, the Black Dog Inn. The black dog figure which sat on top of the inn for almost sixty years, was carved by a father and son team who were both named Arthur Levison. After an absence of thirty years it is good news to hear that Tony Hickman has located the carving and hopes to bring it back to the new Black Dog Inn in the former Shepherd's chemist shop.

Worcester Street c.1907.

Looking up Northgate Street towards St Peters from the top of Worcester Street c.1893.

From the top of Worcester Street to St Johns c.1905 and, opposite, the scene in 1965.

From the corner of Hare Lane to St Peter's church in the late 1910's.

What a charming scene this picture of St Aldate Street makes; a lady with her bicycle deep in conversation with a friend; a group of soldiers in the last year of the Great War crossing the road, heading, perhaps, for the Beaufort Arms; whilst a drover with a cow and calf pass by. Today, standing on the same spot as the photographer, only the kink in the road and the building occupied by Cole & Sons, decorators, would be visible.

Looking the other way, towards Kings Square, a scene lost forever: the Milkmaid Inn, St Aldate Street; the Lamb Inn on the corner of Dog Lane; the Constant's Hotel, Market Parade and the graveyard of St John's church. All have now gone.

Oxbody Lane in the 1890s.

Kings Square in 1965 from the junction with New Inn Lane and King Street, looking towards St Aldate Street. Do you remember this scene with the taxi rank, bus stops, car park, traffic driving round the square, the Regal cinema, Pearce Pope's (auctioneers), the tall trees by the Cattle Market, the Ebenezer chapel next to the new M.E.B. and Bruton Knowles building - Albion Chambers - seen here with sale notices outside?

Four views of Northgate Street. Above, in c.1903. The gentleman in the hat is standing in front of what would today be the Midland Bank.

Could the decorations in this view be for Queen Victoria's Diamond Jubilee in 1897?

On the left is Southern's grocery store, well-remembered by many housewives, seen here in about 1908.

Outside the New Inn in about 1912.

Eastgate Street from the Cross c.1930. Did you ever have to learn those famous lines, 'Out of the night that covers me, Black as the Pit from pole to pole, I thank whatever gods may be, for my unconquerable soul'? The lines were written by that model for Long John Silver, William Ernest Henley, born at 5, Eastgate Street in 1894.

Looking back to the Cross c.1907.

Eastgate c.1895 showing the new Guildhall of 1892 and the original Saracen's Head Inn frontage.

What a change! By c.1909, when this photograph was taken, there has been the addition of better street lighting and electric trams. West of Drinkwater's shop on the right we have Kendall's umbrella manufacturer, who remained here until the early 1960s, the American and Canadian stores and the Rising Sun Inn, later to become the City cinema.

Eastgate c.1927. Do you remember Thomas Cook on the corner of Dog Lane, John Bellows, the printers, and Freeman, Hardy and Willis either side of King Street, Wallace Harris's piano warehouse and Eastmans the butchers?

It was just a short walk down Dog Lane to the Cattle Market, seen here in c.1918. Today it is the bus station.

Clarence Street c.1958. On the one side, the gas office depot, Richard Hall and a row of three storey houses, the first of which was occupied by R.E. Graham, house agent, but in contrast the other side, is little changed today. I wonder how many babies were born at the Gloucester District Nursing Home?

Barton Street, looking towards Eastgate Street from Annandale House, opposite Wellington Street c.1900. The building with the lamps on the extreme right is thought to be the forerunner of T.G. Hall's.

This is the view in the opposite direction c.1928, from the corner of Wellington Street and looking towards Barton gates.

This is a 1922 view of the right-hand side of Barton Street to compare with the photograph on the opposite page.

Barton gates 1947. A house-bound old gentleman I used to visit always greeted me with the words, 'Are Barton gates still there?'. How changed he would find it today!

Barton Street c.1906. I imagine that these two photographs were taken on the same day as the lady on the bicycle appears on both prints - perhaps she was the photographer's wife. The top view is taken from Sinope Street looking towards the India House and the bottom view is taken from just below the Vauxhall Inn (on the left) and the Cromwell's Head Inn on the corner of Millbrook Street.

Gloucester Park main entrance opposite Wellington Street, just before the First World War. The children appear to be in their Sunday best - could it be after morning service? The ornamental arch is still there, but I wonder what happened to the lamp?

The tank in the Park. Having been stripped of its engine, this First World War tank was installed in 1919 near the main Wellington Street entrance. It remained on view until the early years of the Second World War when it fell victim to the 'Scrap for Spitfires' campaign.

A peaceful Brunswick Road with no traffic c.1906. The maid in a gateway appears to be waiting for the milkman whose float is parked on the opposite side of the road by Brunswick Square. Just visible at the end of the road is the Pump Room.

Brunswick Road c.1906 at the junction with Parliament Street. The large trees are in the grounds of Friar's Orchard (the Crypt School) next to the library.

St Michael's Square c.1906.

Queen Street c.1946. I believe the Maison Bond shop to be where Ivor Gurney was born on August 28, 1890.

Two views of Eastgate Street. Above, c.1913, showing, on the right, the City cinema, later to become the Hippodrome in 1915 and Gaumont in 1959. On the left, with a profusion of lamps, is Blinkhorn's shop. Below, c.1927, we have from Queen Street, Parsons ironmongers, Greig's grocers, Harris butchers, Bakers shoe shop, Haywards photography, spectacle and wireless depot, Blinkhorns drapers, furnishers and undertakers, Curry's cycle, gramophone and wireless depot, Eastgate Vaults, the Market House can be seen in its original position, the Capitol and Counties Bank and Botherways restaurant.

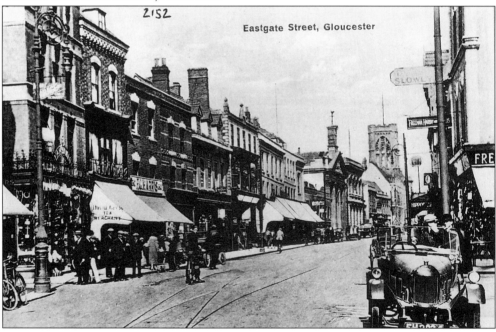

Southgate Street from the Cross in about 1919, showing the bank built in 1895 for the Wilts and Dorset Banking Co., now Burton's, the post office and corn exchange. The corn exchange with the figure of Ceres on top was built in 1895 with a curved frontage. This was altered and straightened in 1893 as can be seen here. It was used for large public gatherings until 1938.

A view from the opposite side of the road c.1907.

This view of the Cross taken from outside the Midland Bank allows us to see how imposing the whole church of St Michael's looked.

An unusual picture of Southgate Street dated 1902. The Bell Hotel has yet to acquire its canopy. The building to the right of Hepworth's is the office of the Gloucestershire Chronicle newspaper which first appeared on 6 July 1833 and continued weekly until 1928. Since the latter was affiliated to conservative politics, whilst the Gloucester Journal was liberal in its bias, modern researchers have alternative contemporary views of events as sources of local opinion for just over a century.

Southgate Street c.1906. Who can resist a photograph of trams?

Southgate Street 1905. The photographer was standing near the Bell Hotel. This was taken prior to the widening of Longsmith Street.

These Southgate Street decorations are probably for the 1911 Coronation of King George V and Queen Mary. The same view today would be from the S.P.C.K. bookshop to the Cross.

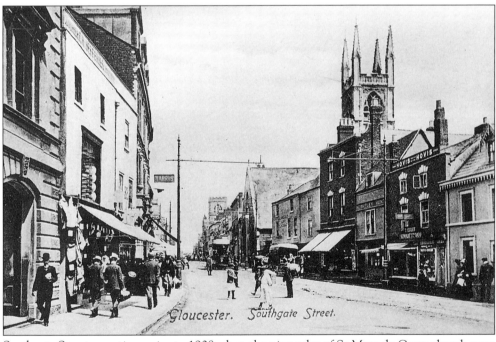

Southgate Street sometime prior to 1908 when the pinnacles of St Mary de Crypt church were removed.

Wet weather and obviously not a very good day for taking a ride in an open top tram! What we have here, though, is a view of the little photographed Kimbrose section of Southgate Street.

This is a view in the opposite direction showing, on the right, the Talbot inn (today, home of the popular broadcasting company, Severn Sound) to Walwins c.1906.

Sudbrook Junction, c.1907, with Bristol Road going off to the right and Stroud Road off to the left. The Kingsholm to Stroud Road tram carries an advertisement for Holloway's - do you remember their lovely leather shop? Between the trams is the Nelson Foster memorial, erected in 1903 and later removed to Sydenham Gardens. The buildings are those of Gee's slate and marble works.

A view of the same junction - this time from Stroud Road - in 1959. The fine redbricked building of the Gloucester Railway Carriage & Wagon Works and the Railway Inn were lost in the last decade to give access to the Peel Centre and an enlarged road junction.

Two
Docks, River and Quay

Sailing ships on the canal in the 1880s.

A view south from Llanthony Bridge c.1890. On the left is the Pillar warehouse and in the distance by the tall ship is Foster Brothers Oil and Cake Mill before the extensions were built in the early nineties.

The west side of the main basin, probably in the 1950s.

Not a soul is about to spoil this tranquil view of the Victoria Dock taken c.1905. There is a good view of the 'new' Custom House opened in 1845 to handle the huge expansion in foreign trade. The building is today the museum of the Gloucestershire Regiment.

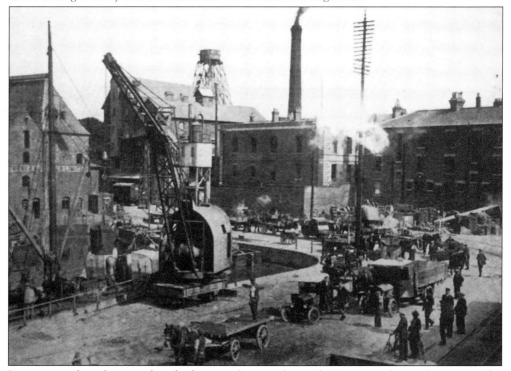

In contrast this photograph, which was taken in the mid-1920s, is a hive of activity. The Stothert and Pitt steam engine is unloading goods to be transported by a waiting queue of horse-drawn and motorized vehicles. In the background is the City Flour Mills (Priday Metford's) and the Custom House. The chimney belongs to the power station on the other side of Commercial Road.

This view from across Victoria Docks in about 1936 shows the extensive warehousing of J.Reynolds & Co., who were famous for their gold medal, award-winning wheatmeal flour.

The City Flour Mills c.1904. This complex of buildings dating from 1850 to 1898 was occupied from 1886 until the late 1980s by Priday, Metford & Co. Ltd.

Two views of Foster Brothers Oil and Cake Mills. Above, the entrance from Merchants Road looking towards Llanthony Road c.1918 and below, a view c.1940, probably taken from Downing's Malthouse showing the sidings of the Midland Railway goods yard, on the site of the old High Orchard dock, in the foreground. In 1899 the firm became one of the original members of BOCM Ltd. Many shiploads of peanuts were handled at the quay, and local children often hung around hoping to scrounge some.

Timber was another commodity which formed a large part of the trade in the docks. Romans had a large timber yard adjoining Llanthony Road.

Looking north across the main basin with the tanker barge Shellmex 7 and three steamers c.1935. On the left are the warehouses along the West Quay (which backed onto Severn Road) demolished in the early 1960s. In the centre is the North Warehouse - today the headquarters of Gloucester City Council.

Biddle and Shipston's warehouses besides the Barge Arms in about 1910, here occupied by the Severn and Canal Carrying Company -the largest in Gloucester. Goods arriving from Avonmouth and the Bristol Channel ports were transferred to narrowboats for distribution via the canal system of the Midlands.

In the 1930's the trade in petroleum developed rapidly. John Harker Ltd operated a number of tanker barges which picked up supplies at Avonmouth and delivered to depots in Gloucester, Worcester and Stourport. This picture shows the motor tanker Whinne H on the Gloucester and Sharpness Canal with part of Price Walker's timber yard behind. The vessel, which carries the sign 'Fina', was built in 1935 and sold in 1959.

We have been very fortunate in recent years to see one or two sailing ships in the docks. How wonderful it must have been to see a crowded basin of working sailing ships like these of the late 1880s.

Fire was an ever-present danger in the docks. The Alexandra Warehouse built in 1870 for corn merchants J.E. & S.H. Fox was badly damaged when, in August 1875, a fire started in the roof and burned slowly downwards. Several manually operated fire engines attended but the jets could not reach the fire. Floors gave way and burning corn poured out of the building making fire-fighting even more difficult. After five hours the fire had burned down to the third storey, which could be reached by the water jets, and the fire was eventually brought under control.

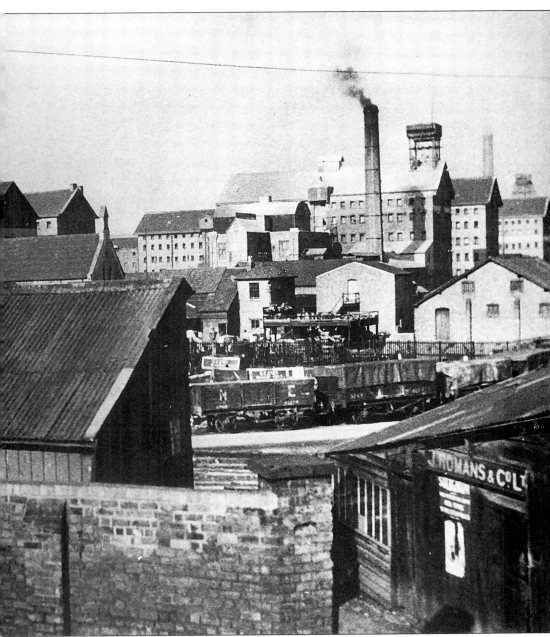

One can sense the atmosphere of the docks from this picture, with the smoking chimney and the many railway trucks, once part of a very extensive railway system. The picture was taken from Llanthony Road, where today visitors enter the docks to visit the Waterways Museum.

To save steel in the First World War concrete barges were built for the Admiralty. Designed to carry 1000 tons of cargo they were built by Hobrough and W.T. Nicholls at a yard just south of Hempsted graving dock. Six were launched the first, Creterock on 23 November 1918, followed by the Creteriver (above), Creteroad, Creteridge, Creteravine and Creterampart.

The Great Western 1899. Captain Howard Blackburn sailed this 30 foot long cutter single-handed across the Atlantic. Departing on 18 June from Gloucester Massachusetts he arrived 61 days later at Gloucester, England. A remarkable feat for a man who had lost all his fingers, half of eachthumb and most of his toes. Several hundred people went to see his tiny craft and many were welcomed on board and offered bourbon whisky and ships biscuits.

The last days of the convict ship exhibition March 1906. 'Success', according to the Gloucester Journal, was built of teak in Burma in 1790, and having served as a merchantman, emigrants' passenger ship to Australia and, finally, a prison ship there, was ending her days as a touring 'convict' ship. On display were approximately seventy cells with wax models of prisoners and a gruesome display of restraints and means of punishment. The exhibition was so popular that it was extended - moving from the main basin to Baker's Quay besides the Pillar warehouse and Downing's malt houses.

The docks have always attracted visitors, whether to see sailing ships, lone sailors, exhibitions or as here, to enjoy a trip on the Wave (above) or her sister ship, the Lapwing for a trip down the canal to Sharpness.

The lock at the quay giving access to the Severn. The Gopsill Brown warehouse is today the very popular Antiques Centre.

Tugs belonging to the Severn and Canal Carrying Company c.1932. The diesel tugs were named Progress and Enterprise and the steam tugs Albert, Active and Victor. They towed groups of barges and long boats up the river Severn to Worcester and Stourport.

The quay in 1909 when a temporary bridge was constructed to give access to the showground of the Royal Agricultural Show which was attended by King Edward VII.

A view from Alney Island looking back at the city towards the quay in c.1903.

Westgate bridge from what was apparently the entrance to Walham path c.1908. The water tank on the right-hand side of the bridge was used for holding river water to be transferred to the Corporation water sprinkler which was used to clean the streets. The tank was removed c.1927. On the left is Price's boathouse.

A picture taken on Westgate bridge looking towards the city showing the Bridge Inn in the centre view and, on the right, a Wickwar sign painted on a building which must be the Foresters Arms.

Three

The 1947 Floods

The 1947 flood was one of the most dramatic in Gloucester's history and certainly the worse this century. After a prolonged period of severely cold weather with snow, on 7 March the snow began to thaw. By 12 March the Severn stood at 17ft 10in (7ft 10in above normal summer height). On 21 March it peaked at 25ft 4in, flooding many houses up to the first floor. The river was within 2in of the top of the quay wall breaking a previous flood record of 1852.

The area flooded was considerable, including Llanthony, the Causeway, Quay and Westgate Street up to St Nicholas' church, St Mary's Street and Square, St Catherine, Worcester, Sweetbriar and Columbia Streets and Deans Walk. The only dry approach from the west was by railway.

Priory Road with Mount Street School in the centre of the picture.

Lower Westgate Street with West Midlands Farmers on the extreme left and the Cooper's Arms, with Mrs Dix at an upstairs window, on the right. The water in the pub was five feet deep. The man holding a small boy is Bill Bell who had a shop next door to the West Midland Association, as it was then called.

Transferring food from one of the four, high level R.A.F. lorries brought in to aid the relief agencies, to a boat to relieve the marooned residents in Westend Parade and Alney Terrace.

The only way to get into the city by road from the west was by means of a diesel lorry which is seen here passing the White Swan Inn.

The Square and Compass Inn at the junction of Westgate Street and Priory Road.

R.F. Meadows' lorry making deliveries. Joe is carrying the sack with brother Freddie standing just behind him. On the planks are the staff of the Co-op. The railings are those by the bus stops.

The Quay. Behind the prison wall the spire of St Nicholas' church and the Barracks can be seen. The eight prison officers' houses (to the left of the wall) built in 1921 were demolished 1985-86 to make way for the new reception and administration block of the prison.

The prison main door in Barrack Square.

One of the Army DUKWS punting up Deans Walk.

A dingy in Deans Walk.

Looking along St Mary's Street towards Westgate Street.

St Mary's Square, south side of St Mary de Lode church with Mrs Price on the extreme left.

St Mary's Square as seen from the junction of the square and St Mary's Street. The group on the plank are left to right Alice Meadows, Maudie Meadows with baby Carol(?), Gordon and Pearl Meadows. In the distance on the plank is Mrs Wellings, and one of the Mayo family can be seen looking out of the window on No. 22.

Planks were used for the bearers and mourners at a funeral at St Mary de Lode church.

Upper Quay Street with the floods up to the milk depot.

Archdeacon Street and the Leather Bottle Inn.

St Catherine Street from St Oswalds Road. The Dymock Flyer, the diesel car which carried rail passengers to Ledbury, passes over the bridge, but Mrs Hackney outside her house on the right-hand side seems more interested in the photographer.

The elderly folk were evacuated from St Bartholomews but most people had to stay in their homes enduring twenty days of flooding. Some houses were flooded to a depth of 10-12 feet and very little in the downstairs rooms was saved. The Flood Relief Committee helped in this austere period after the war to supply the absolute essentials, but it was many months before the houses dried out, were re-plastered, had rotten floorboards replaced and the smell was finally dispersed.

The licensee of the Longford Inn looks pretty despondent - unlike this cheerful band unloading beer barrels at the Queen's Head, Longford.

Four

Transport

Easter traffic April 1927.

A procession in Southgate Street outside the Bell Hotel at the inauguration of horse-drawn trams 26 May 1879.

The Corporation, who wished to extend and electrify the tramway system as far as Hucclecote a rapidly expanding suburb, relaid a new 3ft 6in gauge track. There was obviously great disruption whilst the lines were being laid and the road re-surfaced.

There was a good turn-out to see the new tram leave the Bristol Road depot for its trial run.

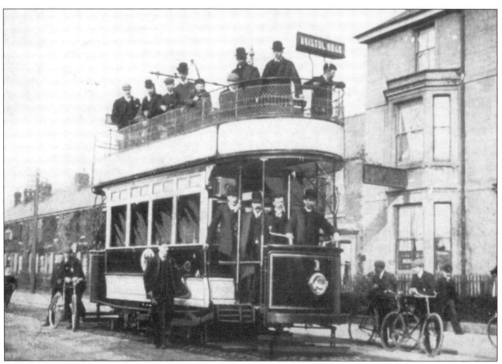

The trial car No. 1 outside the Bristol Hotel. The system opened officially on 27 April 1904 and the fare from the Cross to Hucclecote was 2d. It was not until 1929 that the Corporation replaced most of the tram cars with a motor-bus service.

As a child I often wondered why my elderly relatives called the buses the blue taxis, then I found this early photographof the bus depot in London Road!

Traffic congestion in Westgate Street 1946.

In the 1880s Denton's shop in Northgate Street was probably the largest emporium in Gloucester for ladies' clothes, household and family linens. Here a lady arrives by private transport.

Most people going shopping took a tram like this one which travelled between the Cross and Parkend Road.

Smoke and steam from a railway engine crossing Barton gates c.1906 partially obscures All Saints church. From the left we see Gloucester Coffee House advertising well-aired beds, T.W. Cole tobacconist and newsagent, a horse-drawn cab, and waiting at the gates immediately below the engine's funnel, a Hovis bread cart.

A railwayman with a red flag holds up the traffic at California crossing in Parkend Road for a train to run from the main line to the docks line c.1960-65. This line circled the Park to Sudbrook crossing in Bristol Road into the docks.

The Midland station c.1947. Asda supermarket occupies this site today.

L.M.S. engine No.1537 crossing Llanthony bridge 1936.

The Severn at Westgate bridge. Above, passengers are seen embarking for a river trip on the steam launch Berkeley Castle whilst, below, the River Queen is sailing downstream, approaching the moored rowing boats. It was a very popular activity to hire one of the boats from Price the boat builders who were based at Westgate bridge.

P.V. Taylor's first garage next to the railway bridge in Worcester Street in 1925.

Bristol Road service station in 1968 with a sign up offering pink stamps.

The Albert Motor Co at the Dock gates, Southgate Street c.1912, the sole agents in Gloucester for Skew and Wood Milne tyres.

Westgate Motor House c.1920.

A.C. Stretton, cycle and motor engineers c.1900. The firm was established in 1895 at 103, Westgate Street. This picture shows their new showroom at 2, Worcester Street, next door to Collet's wholesale fruiterers. By 1911 they were agents for Golden Sunbeam, B.S.A., Sparkbrook and Aerial motor-cycles and bicycles, and also stockists of Palmer Cord, Michelin and North British tyres.

Stretton's new garage in about 1930 which was nearer to the railway bridge and is probably better remembered as the Wycliffe garage.

Barnes' garage, Longsmith Street, c.1934.

A line-up of new vehicles for Priday Metford in the docks.

Five

Events

The King's visit in 1909. Here the party is passing the Guildhall.

The First World War was noted for its patriotic fervour. I believe this picture of a recruitment march in Barton Street, past Nettleton Road heading towards Barton Gates, to be one which took place immediately after the Declaration of War on 4 August 1914.

On 2 October 1915 a monster procession was organised to attract the available workforce into the munition factories. Although the procession consisted mainly of men from the Wagon Works and Fielding and Platt, accompanied by floats to illustrate their work, these women (probably from the Quedgeley munitions factory) also paraded. The war work undertaken by women was a major contributor to changing attitudes about their role in society and the emancipation movement. This photograph was taken in Barton Street.

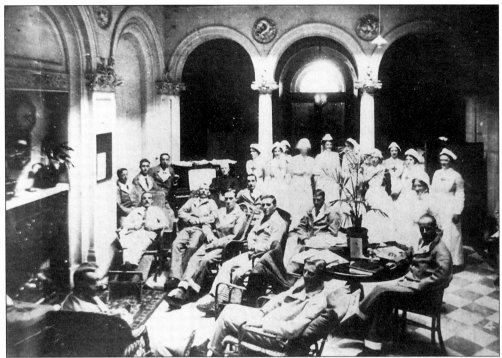

Hillfield House was opened in late September 1915 as a Red Cross Hospital. Dr E.D. Bower (medical officer) and Mrs Nigel Haines (commandant) took in fifty patients in the first week, mostly wounded men from the Dardanelles. The photograph was taken in the central hall used by the soldiers as a day and recreation room.

A tribute to commemorate the War dead on College Green 1922.

A fire-fighting exercise takes place in St Aldate Street in 1940.

The ladies of Fielding and Platt played their part in appealing for others to join them in war work. These patriotic banners evoke the feelings of the times.

Jig and pattern makers for the aircraft industry at Charlesworth, Gloucester 30 May 1945. Back row, left to right: Forest Smith, Edgar Hopkins, Jim Walters, Tom Cook, W. Haynes, Eddy Ede, Frank Cambridge. Middle row: Sid Powell, Len Turk, ? Tarry, Stan Hiam, Les Martin, Eddie Horne, L. Evans, -?-, George Cambridge, ? Williams. Front row: Frank Dudley, R. Smith, A. Teckon, Arthur Elmer, Albert Tarry, Charlie Webber, T. Atwell, Teddy (Ra-Ra) Wiltshire,? Gormley. Sitting on the ground: Judy Harn, -?-.

May 1945 and the end of hostilities. After years of hardship food that had been carefully hoarded was shared to give the children a party. From the many smiles it is obvious that a good time was had by all in St Mary's Square.

The house in St Catherine Street where the first Sunday School opened in July 1780.

The south chapel of St Mary de Crypt church, in Southgate Street which contains tablets and other mementos of Robert Raikes, founder of the Gloucester Journal (first published in 1722) and his son Robert Raikes promoter of Sunday Schools (d.1811).

The house in which Robert Raikes died later to become the base of another printing concern, Crypt House Press in Bell Lane.

Worcester Lawn, Worcester Street, said to be the home of the Revd Thomas Stock, curate of St John's and master of the College School, who, with Raikes, helped develop the Sunday School movement. The house seems to have disappeared around 1912 and the garden, I believe, was occupied by Stretton's garage (later Wycliffe).

I am intrigued to know why an Irishman should have erected this pedestal monument to the Marian martyr Bishop John Hooper in St Mary de Lode church. The Gloucester Journal gives no clue but does give the following description. 'On the east was inscribed John Hooper D.D. Bishop of Gloucester and Worcester was burned on this spot on Saturday Feb. 9 1555 for his steady adherence to the Protestant religion'. On the south side are the arms of the Sees of Gloucester and Worcester impaled. On the north side the bishop's family arms. On the west side 'This monument was erected by James Clealand Esq., of Rath-Gael House, Bangor, Ireland September 1826'. It was replaced by the monument we see today. The picture below shows the crowds who attended the laying of the foundation stone of the monument in 1861, the building of which (but not the figure) was carried out by H. Estcourt.

The Temperance Movement was widely supported and the Bands of Hope promoted the abstainers' cause throughout the city. Here we see a march in 1910 passing down Westgate Street. On the extreme right is Berkeley Street.

This is the Gloucester Band of Hope Union temperance demonstration at the top of Worcester Street marching toward the Kingsholm Football ground 27 May 1911. Whilst the banner reads 'alcohol is poison' and 'our cause is god's' the tram is advertising Godsell's Ales. We also have a good view here of Symond's horse-bus to Norton.

The ceremonial foundation-stone laying for the new Guildhall, Eastgate Street, 23 May 1889. The building, erected at a cost of £30,000, was officially opened on 12 July 1892. It remained the main City Council building until 1986. It is now occupied by the Gloucester branch of the Cheltenham and Gloucester Building Society and the Guildhall Arts Centre.

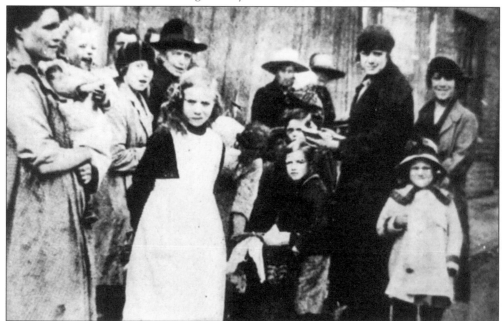

This is April 1925 and what are the ladies buying? Gloucestrians should guess correctly - elvers. How many new housewives and visitors have been teased over the years by being told to chop the head off before cooking this local delicacy.

Mr Embling collecting for charity at the Cross 1927.

One of the 15-16 char-a-bancs and lorries which took the employees of Stephens' vinegar works to Weston-super-Mare in September 1912. The report in the newspaper also tells us that they had to leave at 7 am as it was such a long journey!

Where did everyone flock to on Whit-monday? To the cheese-rolling at Coopers Hill. These pictures are of the 1925 event.

St Michael's School car 'Hong Kong' decorated for the 1910 Empire Day celebrations. Photographed in Russell Street on a wagon loaned by H.C. Morris who had sand and gravel pits.

National School, London Road. These are the hard-working boys who, in 1912, won scholarships which enabled them to receive a free grammar school education. Back row, left to right: Cecil Pullen, Stanley Badham, William Jeffs, Percy Reeves. Seated: Reginald Hyett, Leslie Hopkins, Leonard Barnes, Sidney Ridler.

The Pocket Hercules, as 5 ft tall Eddie Fry was known. He could stretch 10 steel springs of 1200 lb breaking strain, support a 3 cwt anvil on his chest whilst men struck it with 14 lb hammers, lie on a bed of nails with 6 men standing on his chest and allow 6 men to jump on his stomach. A tireless helper of national and local charities he also appeared at the Stage Door Canteen and other theatres.

Hal Bagwell, Gloucester's best known boxer who fought at bantamweight. This photograph taken in 1938 when Hal (right) fought Johnny King (left) at Kingsholm, also shows, left to right: Harry Hemming (King's manager), C.B. Thomas (the famous Welsh referee), Percy Allen and Billy Wagner (Hal's manager, friend, and former West of England middleweight title-holder, also of Gloucester). Hal retired from boxing aged 31, and was licensee of the Lower George, Westgate Street, until 1954.

Six
Buildings

The Kingsholm Inn c.1907.

Lemon and Parkers, Eastgate Street. This well-known watering hole is unusual in having as its name the surnames of its licensees. In about 1882 Arthur Sidney Lemon, a Bristolian, came to Gloucester to take over the business and took into partnership with a Mr Parker who died in 1887. The pub retained its name until it ceased trading in the 1970s. The site is now occupied by Ottakers bookshop.

The Mermaid stood on the Quay at the junction with Quay Street from c.1806 to 1929. On the extreme left is the City mortuary.

The County Shades, Westgate Street. By 1865 the Kings Head, one of Gloucester's premier coaching inns, lost its trade to the railway and was forced to close down, keeping only the bar. It ceased functioning c.1927 and the entire site was demolished in 1944. Today the site is occupied by the Social Services Department office.

Westgate Street, just above Upper Quay Street, at the turn of the century. In the photograph are, R. Meadows and Son, fish and fruit merchants between the Old Bear Inn (left) and the Brewer's Arms, which was supplied by the Crown brewery of Gardner and Branch, St Mary's Street.

The rural setting of the New inn, Stroud Road, Tuffley, only 2 5/8 miles from Gloucester Cross. What a contrast with this road today!

Three Cocks Inn c.1883 when William Preedy was the landlord. It looks a very lawful occasion! I wonder why there are five policemen present?

The Admiral Benbow Inn, Westgate Street which was taken down by the Corporation in 1909 as part of a road-widening scheme.

The Theatre Royal in Westgate Street, which celebrated its centenary with a performance by Henry Irving and Ellen Terry in July 1891. It had many ups and downs in its long history but with the arrival of moving pictures its decline was terminal and on 6 March 1911 it became a cinema. As the very popular Palace cinema (below) it continued until 1922, when the building was sold to Woolworth's who remained there until 1971.

City Cinema, Eastgate Street (constructed on the site of the Rising Sun public house) opened on 20 June 1911. Admission prices were 6d (3p) in the balcony and 3d in the stalls. Following modernisation and the addition of a stage and dressing room facilities it reopened on 1 March 1915 as the Hippodrome.

King's Picture House, Westgate Street, August 1927. A car outside is decorated to advertise the film 'Good Luck'. Converted in 1907 from the Royal Albert Theatre, it was Gloucester's first cinema. It closed on 12 March 1938 and was used as an ARP store during the war. It was finally demolished in 1957 to make way for extensions to the Shire Hall.

The Picturedrome, Barton Street, opened in 1923 and is now the Olympus Theatre. This photograph of the staff about to depart on their annual outing was taken in the late 1920s.

Parkend Empire Cinema, Parkend Road with posters advertising Mary Pickford. This cinema, which opened in 1914 and closed in 1957, is now the Elim Penetcostal church.

The Plaza cinema was opened on 25 November 1935. It was renamed the Odeon in 1957 and converted to a bingo club in 1975.

Northgate Street. The decorated shop fronts of Fry's the baker and confectioner and L.C. Mitchell the electricians, celebrate the Silver Jubilee of King George V in 1935. On the extreme right is Cyril Gabb's butchers shop and on the extreme left Pates, outfitters. The latter's business is still there today.

Sheen's furniture shop standing next to the Theatre de Luxe, Northgate Street, June 1927.

Stephens shop, Worcester Street 1911, decorated to celebrate the Coronation of King George V and Queen Mary.

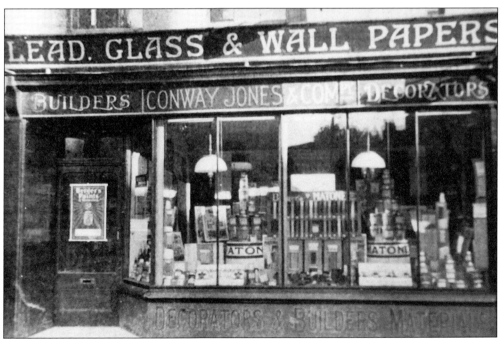

Conway-Jones, the well-known decorator and builders merchant shop, c.1920, which stood in Northgate Street next to the Shakespeare Inn facing Worcester Street.

As Debenham's have just completed a major refurbishment (1995), it is perhaps appropriate to recall this greatest extension made to Bon Marche, as it then was, in the late 1920s, when the Oxbode and Kings Square were created. This photograph looks directly into the old Oxbody Lane from Northgate Street in 1925. The east side is occupied by Brendon Bros and on the other side is Bon Marche's temporary extension which stands where the new Oxbode carriageway now runs.

The Brendon Bros section was replaced by a new building featuring a clock. The picture opposite, c.1929, shows the new store nearing completion except for the part facing Northgate Street.

The 1909 and 1914 sections on the left remain today, the other section was replaced in 1931. The whole building was renamed Debenhams in the early 1970s.

Woodcocks, the well-known cycle shop, in Lower Westgate Street.

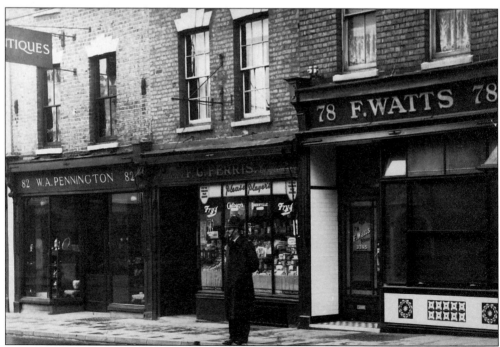

The butchers shop at no. 78 is still there but today it is owned by Ted Harris.

Meadows fish and fruit shop, Westgate Street. The Meadows family have sold fish in the city since 1750. The notice 'The Bloater King still leads the way' refers to Reuben Meadows who had a reputation for supplying the finest Yarmouth bloaters in Gloucester. Reuben had two sons, William who became a carpenter (his son Don was a well-known Westgate greengrocer) and Frederick Charles, known as the 'Elver King', who traded fish around the city. The family now have a stall in Eastgate market headed by Peter and Tim.

The Westend bakery which stood opposite St Bartholomew's almshouses.

The first appearance of Marks and Spencer in Gloucester was in 1912 when a bazaar was opened in Southgate Street. Because of its success this store was later opened in Northgate Street (two doors up from Stead and Simpsons) selling, initially, mainly haberdashery and adding hardware lines later. Textiles arrived in the early 1920s and everything was sold for less than 5/-.

The firm expanded rapidly and became a public company in 1926 and registered its own trade mark, 'St Michael', in 1928. Seeking larger premises in Gloucester in 1931, it purchased the site vacated by Herbert and Sons at 17/21 Northgate Street.

The new Marks and Spencer's store of 8,600 sq ft was opened 11 May 1932.

The opportunity to expand came again in the early 1960s. The first part of the new store opened in May 1963, raising the trading area to 19,000 sq ft - more than a two-fold increase in 30 years.

Eastgate Street showing Maynard's sweet shop, W.H. Smith's and Dewhurst the butchers just before re-building began in 1954.

This photograph of the well-known Gloucester business of Parson Bros, furnishing ironmongers and electricians, also gives us a view up Queen Street, the street in which Ivor Gurney was born.

Ward and Woodman's chemist shop seen here next to Lloyds Bank in Eastgate Street c.1952.

The Gresham Hotel and restaurant in Westgate Street at the junction with Berkeley Street. This was demolished in 1908-9 to make way for the Shire Hall extension.

The bar of the Spread Eagle Hotel in Market Parade.

The City Hotel stood where King Street joined Eastgate Street (where W.H. Smiths now stands). The hotel was occupied at ground level by a grocer with Radbone Andrew, milliners, next door c.1913.

The Wellington Hotel c.1928 when W.A. Johns was the proprietor. The car is parked in George Street facing London Road.

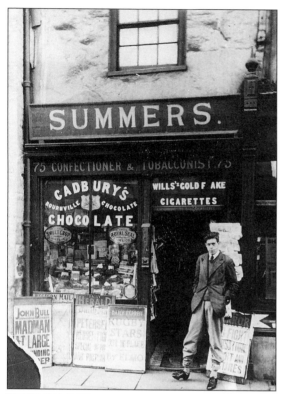

Summers the confectioners and newsagents, 75 Westgate Street. The placard reading 'Petersen v Neusel fight special report and pictures' enables it to be dated c.1935/6. This shop (next to the Old Bear Inn) stood on what is now the open ground in front of the Shire Hall extension.

Gloucester Gas Company offices, which stood facing Brunswick Road replaced Ashmead House. It was Mr Ashmead who developed a variety of apple - appropriately named Ashmead's Kernel - which is still available today.

Christ Church infant's school on the corner of Brunswick Road and Park Road shortly before its closure in 1958. It was opened in the early 1840s as a girls' school and became an infants school in 1931. What a pity we have lost such an elegant building.

Mynd House. The Education Act of 1870 resulted in the provision of primary schools for both sexes. This bow-fronted house in Barton Street, just below Wellington Street, became the Girls' Lower School in 1883. After a move to Bearland in 1904 the school, now a high school, moved to new premises in Denmark Road in 1909.

A fire engine outside the station at Bearland c.1942 which is now the Transport Museum.

Bearland. The county magistrates' courts of 1908 on the corner of Barbican Road and, opposite, Marybone House the former town house of the Hyett family, which became the police station in 1858. Both buildings were demolished to make way for the new police station in the 1960s.

Holtham's veterinary forge, Bearland, stood opposite the Central Police Station (where the Shire Hall car park is today) for over 40 years until Mr Holtham retired in 1922. It then became the blacksmith's forge of Joe Price, the famous strong man of Gloucester. He was the 1922 Amateur weight-lifting champion and took the dead-lift record in 1925 with a lift of 425 lbs. He would demonstrated his ability to write his name on a blackboard with a weight of 56 lbs (1/2 cwt) on his little finger.

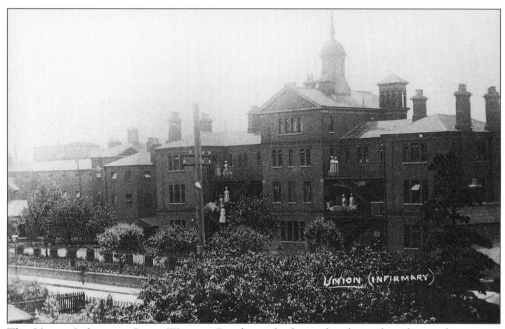

The Union Infirmary, Great Western Road was built in the days when hospital care was provided either by paid subscription or by the local authority. This building stood opposite what is today the Charles Cookson clinic.

The drinking fountain on the Causeway was erected by the temperance societies of Gloucester in July 1911. It was removed in 1971 when the Causeway was reconstructed.

This turn of the century photograph of the Raven Tavern in Hare Lane shows the building prior to restoration and the exposure of its timber-framed structure which is visible today. On the right is College Mews occupied by G. Symonds, job masters and cab proprietors and later demolished to make way for Sainsbury's supermarket.

Northgate Street facing the Oxbode. The two central shops, the glass and china warehouse and W.E. Williams, were demolished c.1912 to make way for a new, mock-Tudor building for Boots the Chemist. The Index shop is here today.

These photographs of Gloucester mothers and theirchidren were taken outside some old town houses in the1890s. It has not been possible to identify their exact location.

These two children were apparently photographed 'in the yard of the Pilgrim's Rest'. New Inn Lane was known as Pilgrims Lane in the eighteenth century, but I have been unable to locate a Pilgrim's Rest in that lane.

I include this charming picture of a group of Gloucester urchins, photographed around the turn of the century because, although I know nothing more about them, it is such an attractive picture in its own right. You may be able to add some more information about them yourself, or indeed about any of the photographs in this book, if you can I would be very pleased to hear of it.

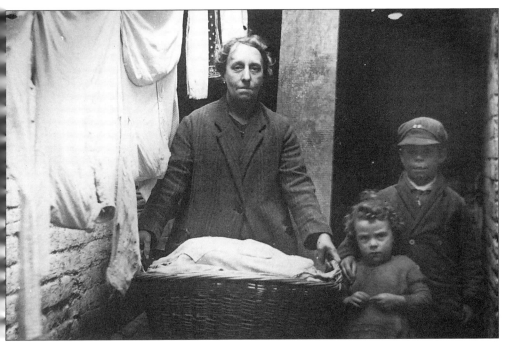

This picture was identified at one of the popular Westenders' exhibitions held at Gloucester Library. It shows Mrs Caroline (Polly) Maisey with her grand-daughter Mildred, aged about three, and Joey Taylor - all from Forester's Yard in Westgate c.1930.

Barbican Place c.1930.

Acknowledgements

I would particularly like to thank Anthony Done for his help and generosity in providing pictures and information gathered during his years of research and photograph collecting. Much of the interesting content of this book arises from his unselfish support. My grateful thanks also to my husband Ron who has spent many hours in the darkroom, rephotographing and enhancing faded photographs for inclusion in this book; to the staff working in the Gloucestershire Collection at Gloucester Library for their unfailing courtesy and helpfulness and to the many people listed below who over many years have so willingly lent me photographs, shared memories and anecdotes, suggested further sources of information and who have been so supportive in the compilation of this volume.

Mrs Jenny James for items on the Walwin negative collection, the Gloucestershire Citizen for photos of Hall Bagwell and the 1947 floods, Hal Bagwell, Mrs Daphne Collier, Hugh Conway-Jones, Mr L.E. Copeland, Brian Frith, Eddie Fry, Harry Greening, Mr G. Hall of Warwick, Mrs Hawkes, Mrs Dot Hawkins, Mr J.R. Hodges, John Jurica, Marks and Spencer plc, especially Janine Johnson and Angela Robertson, Tim Meadows, Forest Smith, Mrs Stephens, Alan Sutton, John Thornhill, Reg Woolford and Hugh Worsnip.